America's
First Ladies
1789 to 1865

The White House in 1820

A Pull Ahead Book

America's First Ladies
1789 to 1865

Lillie Chaffin
Miriam Butwin

Lerner Publications Company   •   Minneapolis, Minnesota

ACKNOWLEDGMENTS: The illustrations are reproduced through the courtesy of: p. 6, Washington and Lee University; pp. 8, 18, 23 (top and bottom), 26, 29 (left and right), 36, 43, 44, 45, 47, 48, 50, 54, 55, 57, 59, 60, 61, 64, 68 (left and right), 70 (left and right), 72, 73, 77, 78, 82, 84, 87, Library of Congress; pp. 9 (left), 65, *Dictionary of American Portraits,* Dover Publications, Inc.; p. 9 (right), National Gallery of Art; p. 11, Society for the Preservation of New England Antiquities; p. 13, Independence National Historical Park Collection; p. 16, Museum of Fine Arts, Boston; p. 20, Pennsylvania Academy of the Fine Arts; p. 25, Amherst College; p. 32, Frick Art Reference Library; p. 37, Metropolitan Museum of Art, Gift of I. N. Phelps Stokes, Edward S. Hawes, Alice Mary Hawes, Marion Augusta Hawes, 1937; p. 40, Ladies Hermitage Association; p. 52, Chicago Historical Society; pp. 69, 76, Smithsonian Institution.

Front cover photo: *Mrs. John Adams* by Gilbert Stuart, National Gallery of Art, Washington, D.C., Gift of Mrs. Robert Homans. Back cover photo: Library of Congress.

Standard Book Number: 8225-0455-3
Library of Congress Catalog Number: 68-31499

Abigail Fillmore

contents

Martha Custis, age 26

Martha Dandridge Custis Washington
(1731-1802)

The daughter of a well-to-do farmer, Colonel John Dandridge, Martha was born in New Kent County, Virginia. She never went to school, but like most young girls, she learned how to sew, cook, spin, weave, and embroider.

Martha was a noted beauty. When she was 18 years old she married Colonel Daniel Parke Custis, a wealthy planter. Seven years later Colonel Custis died, leaving the young widow with two children. A year later she met a handsome young colonel, George Washington, already a veteran of the French and Indian War. They were married in January 1759 at Martha's home. With the children they went to Williamsburg for the rest of the winter. There Washington served his first of many terms in the colonial legislature of Virginia. In April they moved to Mount Vernon.

Washington had lived there for many years, with his half-brother's family, and in 1760 he inherited the estate. For 15 years he worked hard to expand and develop the land. He read books about farming, raised wheat and fruit trees, and marketed the fish from the Potomac. On weekends there were fox hunts at Mount Vernon. Friends from other plantations came to hunt and dance and eat. Washington was a very good dancer.

In 1774 Washington went to Philadelphia to the meeting of the First Continental Congress. The colonies and Britain edged closer and closer to war. In April 1775, war began with the battle of Lexington. In June the Second Congress elected Washington commander in chief of the Continental Army.

Martha shared many of the hardships of war, as she traveled to camps to care for him and to help the ill and wounded soldiers. She was with Washington during the long and painful winter of 1777-1778 at Valley Forge.

The courtship of Martha Custis. Washington became a stepfather to her children, John and Martha. Many years later the Washingtons also raised John's children after he died in the Revolution.

Martha Washington

George Washington (1732-1799)

The next two winters she joined him again at camp in Morristown, New Jersey. At home, she made clothing and other supplies for the soldiers, and watched over the large plantation and its slaves.

Late in 1783, the war over, Washington returned to Mount Vernon. For several years he entertained visitors and developed new and better farming methods. He bred mules, drained swamps, and took up crop rotation. In 1787 he presided over the Constitutional Convention in Philadelphia, and in 1789 the first Electoral College elected him President of the United States.

The first home of the new President was on Cherry Street in New York City. Later, when the government moved to Philadelphia, the Washingtons lived in the elegant home of Robert Morris. A site for the new Federal City had been selected, on a swamp near the Potomac River, and in October 1792 the cornerstone was laid for a white sandstone house.

The Washingtons gave many receptions, and every year on February 22, a birthday ball. Martha was a dignified hostess. Small and slightly plump, she dressed very simply, but her clothes were neat and finely made.

Washington was re-elected in 1793, but by the end of the second term political infighting among his Cabinet members had become intense, and he was relieved and no doubt happy to leave the office to John Adams. Once more a farmer at Mount Vernon, he went often to the Federal City to keep an eye on the building of the new house. He died at the end of the century, on December 14, 1799, and Martha died in 1802. They are buried at Mount Vernon.

Abigail Smith Adams
(1744-1818)

Abigail Smith was born in Weymouth, Massachusetts, the daughter of a minister. Because of ill health, she was not sent to school, but the books in her father's library gave her a fine education. While other children played, Abigail read.

In 1764 she married the young lawyer John Adams, against her family's wishes. They felt that anyone planning to earn a living from other people's troubles was a bad sort. During the next 10 years, five children were born to them.

As a lawyer, Adams was quickly drawn into the mounting conflict with Great Britain. He was elected to the colonial legislature in 1771 and later cheered the action of the patriots at the Boston Tea Party. At the Continental Congresses of 1774 and 1775 he was an early supporter of complete independence from England.

Abigail remained on the farm at Braintree (now Quincy) throughout the Revolutionary War. Adams went to France in 1779 and began a series of negotiations which kept him abroad for almost 10 years. Abigail managed the farm, brought up her children, sewed for the soldiers, and wrote long entertaining letters to her husband. In 1784 she joined him in Paris. When he was appointed minister to Great Britain in 1785, she aided him in his diplomatic work. Abigail had no experience with society, but she met every demand with such tact, simplicity, and sincerity that she did much to close the gap in British-American relations. She did however receive some snubs which she never forgot. Adams himself found the British difficult when it came to making trade agreements, and in 1788, at his own request, they returned to America.

Adams arrived in time for an election. For two terms he served as Vice-President, under Washington, and in 1797 he was elected President. In 1800 the unfinished building in the Federal City — Washington, D.C. — was con-

John Adams (1735-1826). Portrait by Charles Willson Peale. *(Courtesy, Independence National Historical Park Collection)*

sidered ready for occupants. That fall Adams came down to Washington, followed soon after by Abigail in a coach with servants. Workmen had left stacks of equipment and trash in the fields surrounding the house. Inside, it was drafty and cold, and the servants had to hang wet clothes in the East Room for lack of a proper yard. Abigail wrote scornful, half-amused letters about the uncomfortable house, but she was soon able to begin entertaining. She admired Martha Washington's style. With Adams beside her, clad in velvet and bowing to his guests, she held formal receptions in the newly furnished Oval Room.

Adams's term ended in 1801. His years in office had been difficult, for he was caught between members of his own party, the Federalists, who wanted war with revolutionary France, and the rising party of Thomas Jefferson, the Democratic Republicans (later to be called Democrats). Adams avoided war, but he made enemies among both Federalists and Jeffersonians. Hurt and angry, he rushed out of Washington in a coach just before Jefferson's inauguration in 1801. Later, he and Jefferson resumed their old friendship.

Back on the farm at Braintree, Adams studied and read, and wrote statements on public affairs. Abigail became a semi-invalid, but she could still knit, watch over her family and farm, and write letters filled with wit and fine descriptions. Many of her letters have been published, in several notable collections. She lived to see her son, John Quincy Adams, become minister to Prussia, Russia, and England, a United States Senator, and Secretary of State.

Abigail Adams was the only First Lady to be both the wife and the mother of a President of the United States.

Martha Wayles Skelton Jefferson
(1748-1782)

Martha Jefferson did not live to serve as First Lady. The daughter of a wealthy Virginia lawyer, she received an excellent education. At 17 she married Bathurst Skelton. Soon afterward he died, as did their infant son.

Within a few years she met Thomas Jefferson. They were drawn together at first by their love for and accomplishment in music; she played the harpsichord and he the violin. They were married in 1772 and went to live at Monticello, Jefferson's new home, which was still unfinished when they arrived. Jefferson had designed the house and had directed the workmen. The house was built on a hill near Shadwell, his birthplace in the Piedmont region of western Virginia.

Jefferson was a lawyer, and during the 1760's and 1770's — like Adams — he became involved in the colonies' problems with England. He went to Philadelphia as a delegate to the Continental Congress, and in 1776 he wrote the Declaration of Independence. He was not a soldier. He spent the war years in the Virginia House of Delegates, working for democratic reforms in the state government.

Thomas Jefferson (1743-1826). Marble bust by Jean Antoine Houdon. *(Courtesy, Museum of Fine Arts, Boston)*

His two years as governor were more difficult. Virginia was invaded by the British, and in a storm of confused aims and hard feelings, Jefferson resigned. Disgusted with politics, he went back to Monticello.

Martha's health was poor, and she had been an invalid much of the time since their marriage. She had six children, but only two of them, Martha and Mary, lived to adulthood. In September 1782 she died. Jefferson was badly shaken. He talked little, and wrote letters to no one.

He was elected to Congress in 1783, and as a means of distraction, he accepted the job. In 1784 he traveled to France to help Adams and Franklin make trade agreements. Jefferson then became minister to France, and his daughters went to school there. In 1789 they sailed back to America.

Jefferson expected to return to France, but the new President asked him to be Secretary of State. Within Washington's Cabinet, differences of attitude and opinion sharpened, and before the decade was over, parties had formed. Jefferson ran for President in 1796, against Adams; he got three fewer electoral votes and became Vice-President. According to Article II of the Constitution, the Vice-President was the man who came in second. This awkward method of election did not really work for a government with political parties, and it worked even less well in 1800. Jefferson emerged as President from a bitter and confused election. (The 12th Amendment to the Constitution, adopted in 1804, straightened out some of the problems by separating the votes for President and Vice-President.)

The Federalists may have expected revolution and chaos under Jefferson; they feared his democratic beliefs and knew that he sympathized with revolutionary France.

Martha Jefferson Randolph (1772-1836), Jefferson's daughter, occasionally acted as his hostess in the White House.

The Federalist party itself began to fall apart, but Jefferson's government ran along more smoothly than his enemies expected. The democratic and French influences were felt — and tasted — in his household. He put an end to the courtly receptions of Washington and Adams, and he shook hands with guests, rather than bowing. Small dinner parties gathered at a round dining table so that nobody could lead the way. The food was French. Jefferson kept a good stock of imported wines and a French chef.

At first, Jefferson lived alone in the White House, with only a mockingbird and his servants. Dolley Madison, wife of the Secretary of State, acted as his hostess. In 1802 his daughters, both married, came to visit; and during his second term, after Mary's death, Martha often spent winters with her father. She had six children, and her seventh, James Madison Randolph, was born in the White House.

In 1808 Jefferson's good friend Madison became President. Jefferson, with relief and anticipated pleasure, went back to Monticello, and Dolley Madison became First Lady in her own right.

Portrait by Gilbert Stuart. *(Courtesy, The Pennsylvania Academy of the Fine Arts.)*

Dolley Payne Todd Madison

(1768-1849)

Dolley Payne was born of Quaker parents in North Carolina. She grew up in Scotchtown, Virginia, and moved with her parents to Philadelphia in 1783, when she was 15. There she met and married John Todd, a lawyer. Todd and one of their two sons died during the yellow fever epidemic of 1793.

During the 1790's Philadelphia was, briefly, the nation's capital. Congressmen were to be found at every gathering. Dolley met Representative James Madison from Virginia, and in 1794 she married him. Madison was 17 years older than Dolley, and he was not a Quaker. Because of this, Dolley had to drop her religion. The switch from Quaker gray did not, it seems, displease her.

Dolley, who loved to entertain, soon became a social leader in Philadelphia. She was warm, friendly, and tactful, quick to learn names and faces, and unwilling to quarrel or gossip. These qualities made her a great asset to her quiet, scholarly husband.

Madison's knowledge of history and government had made him perhaps the most useful man at the Constitutional Convention of 1787. There he worked out a structure for the new government, and later as a member of Congress he prepared the Bill of Rights. In 1797 the Madisons made a brief escape from politics. They went back to Montpelier, his estate in Orange County, Virginia. But the Alien and Sedition Acts of 1798 drew him back. With Jefferson he opposed these Federalist-sponsored laws restricting the freedom of speech and press. In 1801 Madison became Jefferson's Secretary of State, and Dolley began her career as a White House hostess.

Not until 1809 did she have full command in the White House. At Madison's inauguration ball she appeared in a gown of cream-colored velvet, with a long train, and a matching turban trimmed with white satin and ostrich feathers. Most of Dolley's clothes came from Paris. It was not easy to get them. Britain and France were at war, and when Britain blockaded the French coast, Dolley had to send special requests to the wife of the American minister in France. Flowers and feathers, stockings and gloves were to be sent "on a safe vessel" back to Washington.

A new state coach was purchased in Philadelphia. Every afternoon Dolley climbed into the fine brown coach, sat back against cushions edged with yellow lace, and raced through the muddy streets of Washington to pay calls.

Dolley put an end to the Jeffersonian ruling against a weekly reception. Aided by a French steward, she gave an unending series of teas, dances, lawn parties, and dinners. Whether or not Dolley Madison was a great beauty may be argued, but there is little question that she charmed and amused her guests. At some of her parties she glided about with a romantic novel in hand. To entertain a shy guest, she would read aloud a favorite passage.

British troops burn Washington, August 1814.
Below, the White House after the fire.

Now and again, Madison himself would amuse his guests with a clever phrase, but he grew more quiet and distant as war with Britain approached. The country was divided: a group called the War Hawks clamored for battle while Federalist merchants in New England did not want to lose the English trade. On June 18, 1812, at Madison's request, Congress declared war.

For two years the war sputtered along, chiefly near Canada and the Great Lakes. In Washington the parties continued though Madison grew more pale and tense. In late August 1814 the British invaded Maryland. They were on the way to Washington when Madison got on his horse and went off to join the militia guarding the city. Dolley was left in the White House with her French steward and a few frightened servants. She packed the cabinet papers into a trunk, and began to write a long letter to her sister.

At sunrise on the 24th she went up to the roof and through a spyglass watched the British send the local militia flying in all directions. By afternoon she knew the victory dinner she had planned would go uneaten. Her carriage waited as she tore the portrait of Washington out of its frame. She finished the letter to her sister, and was on the road to Virginia when British troops arrived in Washington. At the White House they ate the dinner Dolley had left, then piled up the chairs and tables and set them on fire.

James Madison (1755-1836)

The burning of Washington was followed by a hurricane. Roofs flew off houses, and torrents of rain put out the fires. When the Madisons came back, the blackened, gutted White House walls remained but the roof was gone.

Workmen began to make repairs, but the Madisons never lived there again. They moved into a private home and Dolley began to give parties once more. The war ended with a treaty signed at Ghent, Belgium, in December 1814.

In 1817 the Madisons went back to Montpelier. Madison died in 1836, and Dolley returned to Washington. She took a house on Lafayette Square and entered society again. Congress gave her free postage and a seat in the House of Representatives, and bought her husband's papers and letters. The last pleasant years at Montpelier had cost a great deal.

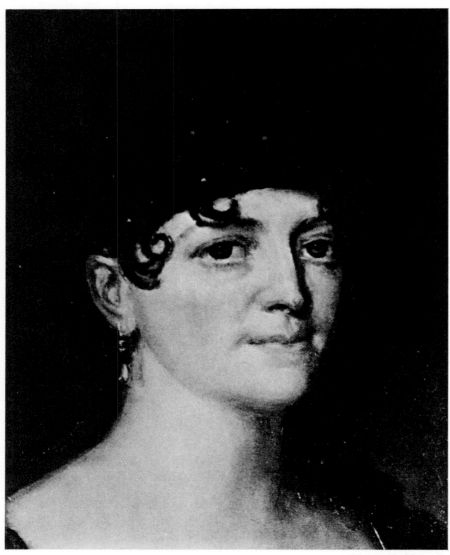

Elizabeth Monroe

Elizabeth Kortwright Monroe
(1768-1830)

Elizabeth Kortwright grew up in New York City. Her father, who had retired as an officer in the British army, was a wealthy merchant. In 1786, when she was 17, she married James Monroe, a young lawyer from Virginia. They settled in Fredericksburg, where Eliza, the first of their two daughters, was born.

Monroe had studied law under Thomas Jefferson and at the time of his marriage had already served in the Virginia assembly and in the Continental Congress. Monroe admired Jefferson and followed his political principles closely, sometimes more closely than Jefferson did. Because Monroe did not believe in a strongly centralized government, he at first opposed the new Constitution. But he entered national politics with gusto during the first Washington administration. As Senator from Virginia he lined up with Madison and Jefferson and was a sharp critic of Hamilton.

The Monroes moved to Charlottesville in order to be close to Jefferson at Monticello. They built a home called Ash Lawn. After 1794, however, they were not often at home. Monroe became minister to France, and Elizabeth went along. After a brief stay in Virginia, as governor, he went back to Europe in 1802 on diplomatic missions for

Jefferson. In Paris, Monroe gave Robert Livingston the go-ahead to buy a huge chunk of land that Napoleon had offered to America. Jefferson expected only New Orleans, and received instead the whole Louisiana territory. But most of Monroe's attempts at treaty-making did not work out so well. Elizabeth went with him to London and found the damp weather disagreeable. The British attitude toward trade agreements was equally unpleasant, and in 1807 the Monroes came back to the United States.

The years abroad had given them a chance to take a long hard look at court manners. Monroe was impressed. When he was elected President in 1816 he told Elizabeth that it would be a good idea to reorganize the White House social calendar. No more diplomats casually dropping in whenever they liked; no more of this gay bouncing about Washington to pay calls, which Dolly Madison had seemed to enjoy so much. In European courts the business of receiving guests was highly organized. There were rules to follow. The Monroes would now provide the new nation with an example of correct social behavior.

For nine months after the inauguration they lived in a private home while workmen cleaned and painted the rebuilt White House. The Monroes furnished the house with some of their own French furniture as well as with elegant new pieces ordered from France. On January 1, 1818, they held their first reception.

Soon after, the new social system went into effect. Elizabeth Monroe would not pay calls. Word went out that she was in weak health, and that her married daughter Eliza Hay would return calls — but would never be the first to call. Eliza had grown up in Europe and was quite sure she knew the proper way to treat a diplomat. Now she began to dominate social planning in the White House. For every occasion she had a list of rules based upon her awareness of rank. People soon assumed that she and her mother were enormous snobs. Eliza probably was.

James Monroe (1758-1831) and his daughter Eliza Hay. John Quincy Adams referred to Eliza as an "obstinate little firebrand."

By autumn of 1819 most of the women in Washington refused to go to White House gatherings, though Elizabeth Monroe's sisters could always be counted on. In 1820 the Monroes' younger daughter Maria was to be married in the White House. Eliza took charge. Neither Cabinet members nor diplomats were to be invited. A small wedding may have been pleasant for 16-year-old Maria, but being dragged into Eliza's feud with the diplomats was not.

Now and then the Cabinet had to interrupt its work to consider fine points of etiquette brought up by Eliza, and Secretary of State John Quincy Adams spent a lot of time soothing diplomats whom she had snubbed.

Monroe was not opposed for re-election in 1820. The Federalist party had folded up. The years of Monroe's presidency are often called "the era of good feeling" because there was only one political party. But within that party people began to take sides. The Democratic Republicans had always quarrelled among themselves, but their voices grew louder after 1820, when war hero Andrew Jackson began to attract a following.

During Monroe's second term, however, good feelings were more evident in the White House. Eliza's behavior did not change, but people realized that her mother was not entirely to blame for the cold dull parties and the offended diplomats. After 1820 more and more people came to Elizabeth's receptions. On one occasion Monroe received a visit from six Indian chiefs who brought with them three squaws and a small child. They conversed in five Indian languages, French, and English. The Indians were almost entirely bare, but for paint and beads. A few days later when they came back to see Monroe again, someone — perhaps Adams — had dressed them in suits of store-bought clothes.

After the tight election of 1824 was settled in the House of Representatives, everybody came to mill about at Elizabeth Monroe's last reception: Adams the President-elect, Clay, Webster, Calhoun. Somebody picked the pocket of General Winfield ("Old Fuss and Feathers") Scott. But the center of attention was Andrew Jackson.

In 1825 the Monroes went back to Oak Hill, their new Virginia home. Elizabeth died in 1830 and was buried there. Monroe, who had run out of money and was too old to practice law, went to live in New York. He died there in 1831.

Louisa Johnson Adams
(1775-1852)

Louisa Adams is the only First Lady who was born abroad. Her father, Joshua Johnson, was an American from Annapolis, Maryland, whose business took him to England, and her mother was an Englishwoman. During the American Revolution, when Louisa was two years old, her family moved to France. After the war they went back to England where her father became American consul general. In 1795 Louisa met John Quincy Adams, a young diplomat. Adams was American minister to The Netherlands, and he had come to London on a special assignment. He and Louisa were married in 1797, and after three months in England they set off for Berlin. John Adams had just appointed his son minister to Prussia.

John Quincy's diplomatic career had begun very early. He was not quite 11 in 1778 when his father was sent to Paris to negotiate with the French and the British. He begged to go along, and his father took him. He went to schools in France and in Holland, studying the classics and French, dancing and fencing, and at 14 was ready for his first assignment, a trip to Russia with diplomat Francis Dana. In St. Petersburg he acted as Dana's private secretary and interpreter of French. Back in Paris, he was his father's secretary during the final negotiations with Britain. When John Adams became minister to Britain after the war, John Quincy went home to Harvard.

President Washington sent him to The Netherlands in 1794, and for the next 30 years Adams's chief work was as a diplomat. When Jefferson was elected President, John Adams ordered his son to come home from Prussia. The trip back to Boston in 1801 was Louisa's first visit to the United States.

Her marriage to Adams was not a love match, but it was, according to Adam's diary, "satisfactory." She had four children, a daughter who died in infancy, and three sons, two of whom died as young men. Louisa's health was weak, and she always found northern cities, including Boston, difficult to live in.

In 1803 Adams was elected to the United States Senate. He was thought to be a Federalist but he supported some of Jefferson's policies, and the Federalists in Massachusetts became very angry. They booted him out of the party and took his Senate seat from him before his term expired. Later Adams went to a Democratic Republican caucus, and worked under Presidents Madison and Monroe. But he was a crusty, independent man. He disliked political parties and tried to remain apart from them — no very great difficulty, for his harsh manner did not win great numbers of people to his side.

He was however a skilled diplomat, and in 1809 Madison appointed him minister to Russia. Adams and Louisa left their two older boys at school and took off for St. Petersburg with little Charles Francis. At the age of two another Adams began his travels. Like his father, he was to become a great diplomat.

In Russia Adams found that he hadn't enough money to entertain in the grand manner of the European diplomats. This may have been at times embarrassing, but it gave Adams a chance to study and to go to museums. Louisa, of course, was miserably cold.

In the spring of 1814 Adams left his family in Russia and went to Ghent, where he was to head the American delegation at a treaty conference. For months he handled difficult negotiations with the British, in an effort to end the War of 1812. Every night Henry Clay and the other Americans drank and played cards, sometimes till dawn. Adams always liked a glass of good wine, but obvious boozing got on his nerves. It was hard to stay on good terms with the other Americans, but his treaty with the British was a very good one. America came out of a rather pointless war without losing territory to the British.

The treaty was signed in December 1814, and Adams went to Paris to join Louisa and Charles Francis, who had made a wild trip by coach across Europe. Napoleon's troops were still fleeing from Russia and in one village they stopped her coach, thinking that it carried Russians.

From France the family went to England, where Adams was minister for two years. In 1817 James Monroe asked him to be Secretary of State, and they sailed for home.

This too was a diplomatic post, but it edged toward the political, for Adams knew that three Secretaries of State — Jefferson, Madison, and Monroe — had become President.

A reception given by John Quincy Adams (right) for Senator Andrew Jackson (center).

Adams worked hard. He dealt with the problems created by the Monroe ladies (Louisa too would only *return* calls, not make them first); he bought Florida from Spain; and he wrote some notes on Latin-American relations which became the Monroe Doctrine. By 1824 he assumed that the presidency would seek him. Of course he did not campaign.

Although Andrew Jackson won the most popular votes, none of the four candidates received a clear majority of the electoral votes. On February 9, 1825, the House of Representatives had to decide which of the first three would be President. Clay, the fourth, threw his votes to Adams.

President Adams named Henry Clay his Secretary of State, and the Jacksonians, already angry, went into a rage. They were sure that a deal had been made. Adams denied the charge but the Jacksonians did not believe him. In Congress they fought every measure he introduced, and began the 1828 campaign early.

John Quincy Adams (1767-1848). Daguerreotype portrait by Southworth and Hawes, 1848. *(Courtesy, The Metropolitan Museum of Art)*

At the White House, Louisa pulled herself together and was able to be a good hostess in spite of her illness. She gave several splendid parties for the Marquis de Lafayette who paid a long visit in 1825. Lafayette, who traveled around the country and received gifts everywhere, was allowed to keep his pet alligator in the East Room.

Most of the White House dinners were a bit dull. Adams could not make small talk and was too shy to converse much in the company of a large number of people. Close friends knew that he could talk well about subjects that mattered to him.

Adams may also have been tired at late dinners. Every day he got up before dawn, wrote in his diary, and took a long walk, alone, through Washington. Sometimes he rode horseback or swam in the Potomac. At sunrise he came back to the White House, read the Bible, and had breakfast. Then he went to his office to meet a long stream of visitors till late afternoon.

Though Adams's program to advance science and agriculture failed in Congress, he was able to make a good deal of progress on the White House lawn. He worked closely with his gardener who planted flowers and vegetables and countless seedlings for trees. Adams, in fact, counted them; and late in his term he sometimes spent hours in deep thought among the poppies, herbs, and wild cherries. Even the weeds pleased him.

Louisa too preferred her garden to the Oval Room. Among the quiet flowers she could sew, read, and draw, with one eye on a growing family of silkworms.

The noisy, bitter election of 1828 ended the Adamses' stay in the White House. The Democratic Republican party had split wide open. Jackson won, and his followers shortened the party name to *Democratic.* In the 1830's supporters of Adams and Clay and others who opposed Jackson would form the Whig party.

Adams did not attend Jackson's inauguration, but he and Louisa remained Washingtonians. In 1830 he was elected to the House of Representatives by the people of Plymouth, Massachusetts. For 17 years he served in the House, after 1836 without party designation. Free to follow his conscience, he fought against the Gag Rules which cut off debate about slavery. Like many other Americans he questioned America's part in the Mexican War. On February 21, 1848, Congress was about to award hononary swords to the winning generals. Adams protested against this attempt to glorify a "most unrighteous war." Before he could vote, he had a stroke and slumped to the floor. Louisa was called, but he lost consciousness before she arrived. Two days later he died in the Speaker's room.

Rachel Jackson

Rachel Donelson Robards Jackson
(1767-1828)

Rachel Donelson was born in Virginia and grew up in frontier settlements of Kentucky and Tennessee. Her father, Colonel John Donelson, was one of the founders of Nashville. When Rachel was 17 she married Captain Lewis Robards, an army officer. The marriage was brief and unhappy, and Rachel returned to the boardinghouse of her widowed mother. There she met a boarder, Andrew Jackson, who had come to Nashville from North Carolina to be attorney general in the Tennessee territory.

To escape from the quarrelsome Robards, Rachel went to Natchez, Mississippi. Jackson joined her there. They heard reports that Robards had got a divorce, and in 1791 they were married. Two years later, in December 1793, they found out that Robards had only got the divorce three months before. To make sure that everything was in order, they were married again, in Nashville, early in 1794. In later years this confused order of events gave people who liked to gossip something to gossip about, and eventually it became a subject for political slander.

Jackson — born in a log cabin — had become an orphan at 14. After his marriage he began to buy land and to sell it to settlers at a very good price. In 1796 he bought some land of his own, a plantation called the Hermitage, not far from Nashville.

In 1797 Jackson appeared briefly in both the House and the Senate, but he found Philadelphia a slow dull town and went back to Tennessee. There he served for a time as a state judge. He also ran two plantations, a general store, and a stable of race horses. His frequent duels kept Nashville from becoming a dull town.

The Jacksons had no children, but they raised three of Rachel's nephews as well as the son of another nephew. Rachel—whose honor was often the subject of Jackson's duels—lived very quietly. She stayed at home, read her Bible, and chatted with friends. But Jackson himself was soon to receive wide public attention. He went into the War of 1812 a major general in the Tennessee militia and came out the hero of the battle of New Orleans. The treaty of Ghent had been signed two weeks before the battle ended, but news traveled slowly. On February 11, 1815, Washington heard about Jackson's victory, and three days later about Adams's treaty. To succeed in war and peace at the same moment delighted many Americans. They heard of Jackson again when he defeated the Seminole Indians of Florida in 1818.

Well before the 1824 election Jackson was thought to be presidential material. The Tennessee legislature put up his name in 1822 and then elected him to the Senate. After the Adams victory in the House, Jackson resigned his Senate seat and lay low, waiting for 1828.

Andrew Jackson (1767-1845)

Although differences of political opinion divided the Democratic Republican party, the election of 1828 was really a battle of personalities. Adams the New Englander of old family was confronted by the westerner Jackson — wealthy indeed — but born in a cabin. The wives of both candidates were up for attack in the press: Louisa Adams for being an Englishwoman, Rachel Jackson for graver sins by far — her divorce and remarriage.

Jackson won the election but Rachel did not become First Lady. In December 1828 she went to Nashville to shop with friends. In the Nashville Inn she heard women's voices talking in loud whispers about her. She broke up. Her friends took her back to the Hermitage, where on the night of December 22 she died of a heart attack.

Jackson's first reception at the White House,
as seen by British artist Robert Cruikshank.

When Jackson appeared in Washington before his inauguration he was not in a mood to forgive anyone. He
didn't call on President Adams, and Adams was probably
wise to make a quick and graceful escape. Inauguration
Day was Jackson's alone. Mobs of people poured into
Washington. They cheered and shouted, and hurried to

the White House for ice cream and cake and a good look at Jackson. They jumped on tables, dropped china, pulled and tore the curtains. Jackson made a safe getaway. He stepped out of a window, and went to spend the night at Gadsby's Hotel.

Early in his term Jackson began to redecorate the White House. James Monroe had bought back many of his furnishings and by 1828 the place seemed shabby. New furniture, chandeliers, carpets, and mirrors made the house splendid and erased the last hint of John Quincy Adams. On the south lawn Jackson planted magnolia trees to remind him of Rachel.

Emily Donelson, Rachel's niece, acted as Jackson's hostess. In the winter of 1837, Emily went home to Tennessee, where she died of consumption before Jackson returned from Washington.

Emily Donelson, Rachel's niece, became Jackson's hostess, and her husband (a Donelson nephew), Jackson's secretary. Their four children were born in the White House. In 1830 the Donelsons went back to Tennessee for several months to avoid the presence of Peggy Eaton at White House parties. Peggy was the wife of the Secretary of War; a tavern keeper's daughter, she had married Eaton when her sailor husband died at sea. Because of this doubtful past, the Cabinet wives snubbed her. Jackson was reminded of the attacks upon his wife, and he defended Peggy against all comers, including John Calhoun. Mrs. Calhoun, enraged by Peggy, went back to South Carolina; and Calhoun himself soon split with Jackson on the tariff issue. The high tariffs of 1828 and 1832 hurt the South and angered Calhoun, who said that if a state (namely, South Carolina) did not like a federal law, that state could disregard it. In 1832 Calhoun resigned the vice-presidency and entered the Senate to continue his argument.

Martin Van Buren, who liked Peggy Eaton, had already replaced Calhoun on the ticket for the election of 1832, and four years later with Jackson's support he became President.

Hannah Hoes Van Buren
(1783-1819)

Hannah Hoes was born in the little Dutch village of Kinderhook, New York, where she grew up with her distant cousin Martin Van Buren. They went to school together and liked many of the same things. At 14 Martin began to study law with a local attorney. He finished his studies in New York City and went back to Kinderhook to begin practicing law. He and Hannah were married in 1807.

Martin Van Buren
(1782-1862)

Van Buren admired Thomas Jefferson and entered politics as a Democratic Republican. He was elected to the New York senate in 1812 and moved his family to Albany, the state capital. Hannah was pleased about the election but she did not like city life. Her health became poor and she died at the age of 36, soon after the birth of her fourth son. Van Buren never remarried.

At the time of Hannah's death, in 1819, Van Buren was attorney general of New York. In 1820 his candidate for the United States Senate defeated Governor Clinton's, and Van Buren's political life began to swing. He was elected to the Senate and continued to guard New York politics through a group called the Albany Regency. (A well-run political machine, the Regency controlled the Democratic party in New York State from 1820 until 1842.)

Van Buren supported Jackson in 1828 and became his Secretary of State. He was a tactful, courteous man and didn't find it a strain to be nice to Peggy Eaton. In 1831 when Jackson asked the Senate to confirm Van Buren as minister to Great Britain, he missed by one vote. That vote was John Calhoun's.

Jackson and Van Buren defeated Henry Clay in the election of 1832, and in 1836 Van Buren faced William Henry Harrison, the candidate of the newly formed Whig party. Van Buren won. In March 1837 Jackson went back to Tennessee, cheered loudly by crowds. In May financial panic broke out, largely as a result of wild speculation in public lands. People had bought land that didn't exist and had paid for it with money they didn't have.

Following his Jeffersonian beliefs, Van Buren said that there was very little the federal government could do about the depression. He did cut back the number of White House parties. He gave small dinners and only an occasional reception. By 1838 Washington society felt cheated. Dolley Madison decided that what the White House really needed was a hostess. Her young relative, Angelica Singleton of South Carolina, had just finished school in Philadelphia.

Angelica Singleton Van Buren was hostess for her father-in-law.

Dolley introduced her to Van Buren's eldest son, Abraham, and they were married in time for Angelica to greet guests with her father-in-law at the New Year's reception of 1839.

Hard times made enemies for Van Buren on every side. In 1840 the Whigs nominated Harrison again and put on a wild campaign. Reaching for the Jacksonian common man, they attacked Van Buren for his elegant manners and gilded dinnerware. Harrison won.

Van Buren went back to New York and found the Albany Regency about to split into two factions, the Barnburners and the Hunkers. Van Buren entered the battle on the side of the radical Barnburners. In 1848 he was again a presidential candidate, running on the Free-Soil ticket with Charles Francis Adams. Afterwards, Van Buren returned to the Democratic fold, but he continued to oppose slavery. He died in 1862 and was buried next to Hannah in Kinderhook.

Anna Symmes Harrison
(1775-1864)

Anna Symmes was born in Morristown, New Jersey, where her father was a judge. Her mother died shortly after Anna's birth, and the child was taken to a grandmother who lived on Long Island. When her father remarried and moved to North Bend, Ohio, as a state supreme court judge, Anna went with him.

In this little frontier town she met William Henry Harrison, a captain who commanded the military post of Fort Washington, Ohio. Harrison was a Virginian, born at Berkeley, a plantation about 20 miles from Richmond. In 1791 his father's friend, George Washington, had agreed that William should drop medicine as a career and join the army. His first assignments were in the Indian wars, and in 1794 he came to Fort Washington. Anna's father objected that Harrison could not support a wife, but Anna paid no attention. They were married in November 1795.

Five years later Harrison, who had resigned from the army, was appointed governor of the Indiana Territory, and they moved to Vincennes where he built a fine home. Anna gave birth to 10 children, six of whom died before Harrison became President.

Tecumseh, chief of the Shawnee Indians, offers a warning to Governor Harrison. Tecumseh believed that the Indians held their land in common and that an individual tribe could not sell or give away its land. *(Courtesy, Chicago Historical Society)*

As governor, Harrison made a treaty in 1809 with several Indian chiefs who agreed to turn over a large portion of land to white settlers. Other Indians disliked the treaty and refused to leave the territory. Their leader was Tecumseh, a skilled fighter, speaker, and organizer. Tecumseh was off on a trip to organize southern tribes when his brother, the Shawnee Prophet, was confronted by Harrison and the territorial militia. At dawn on November 7, 1811, the Prophet and his warriors attacked the militia. For two hours they fought in a slow cold rain before the Indians were routed. Then Harrison's men destroyed the Shawnee village on the banks of the Tippecanoe River. It is not clear whether the battle of Tippecanoe was a decisive victory, but from it Harrison gained a campaign slogan and the presidency.

The Indians had been partially supplied by the British, whom they joined in battle during the War of 1812. Harrison entered the army again and was given command of troops in the Old Northwest. In 1813 he defeated the British near the Thames River in southern Ontario. Among the enemy dead was Tecumseh, a brigadier general in the British army.

During the war Anna returned to her father's home in Ohio, and later Harrison joined her there. In 1814 they moved to a farm near North Bend and for the next 20 years Harrison made occasional excursions into public office, including the United States Senate.

In 1836 the Whig party could not decide whether to nominate Henry Clay or Daniel Webster. As a compromise they selected Harrison. Van Buren won the election, but in 1840, sniffing victory, the Whigs again put up Harrison. To widen their appeal, they tacked on an ex-Democrat from Virginia, John Tyler, as his running mate. The Whigs could not agree on a platform but they did have a slogan: "Tippecanoe and Tyler too."

William Henry Harrison (1773-1841)

After warning Harrison to avoid making statements about his political aims, the Whigs put on a great show. Harrison the frontiersman, the Indian fighter, and the Ohio farmer was set up against President Van Buren. Forgotten was Harrison the gentleman from Virginia. Log cabins and cider barrels and torchlight parades brought victory to Harrison — and Tyler.

The campaign did not convince Anna Harrison that her husband should be President. Her health was poor, and in March 1841 she stayed at home in North Bend and sent her daughter-in-law Jane to Washington.

A few days before the inauguration the newspapers announced that Harrison would not be able to shake hands

Anna Harrison. Her son John was the father of Benjamin Harrison, President of the United States from 1889 to 1893.

at the ceremony, or afterwards. His hand was sore from campaigning. But he was able to make a two-hour speech in freezing rain.

He caught a cold and was given no chance to rest. Swarms of office-seekers hit him for jobs, and Harrison, handkerchief in hand, found it hard to escape them. One day late in March he went to a market to shop for vegetables. It was raining again and his cold became worse. On April 4, 1841, he died of pneumonia.

He was given a splendid funeral. Newspapers said that the procession was more skillfully organized than his inauguration parade. Anna Harrison had been First Lady for 31 days, and had not reached the White House. Twenty-three years later she died in North Bend.

Letitia Christian Tyler
(1790-1842)

Letitia Christian was born in New Kent County, Virginia, near Richmond. Her father, a wealthy planter, guarded his daughter closely and refused to allow her to marry John Tyler until they had been engaged five years. The marriage took place in 1813, when they were both 23. They moved to a small farm and when John's father died, they took over the large Tyler plantation in Charles City County. Letitia had eight children — five daughters and three sons.

At the time of their marriage, Tyler was a lawyer and member of the Virginia House of Delegates. In 1816 he was elected to the House of Representatives, and in 1825 he became governor of Virginia. Two years later he entered the Senate.

Tyler clung tightly to his Jeffersonian principles and opposed any bill that hinted at federal power over the states. But the tariff crisis of the 1830's trapped him. He attacked South Carolina for trying to strike down the federal tariff, but he was even angrier when Jackson tried to force South Carolina to accept the law. A compromise tariff cooled things off, but Tyler resigned from the Senate. As an anti-Jacksonian he assumed that he should join the Whigs.

Letitia Tyler

In 1840 that party chose Tyler to run for Vice-President with Harrison. Nobody paid much attention to him during the campaign, and afterwards he expected to lead a quiet life in Virginia, with an occasional trip to Washington when the Senate met. A cold damp March took care of William Henry Harrison, and the Tyler family came up from Virginia and moved into the White House.

Letitia Tyler had suffered a stroke in 1838, and throughout her White House stay she was confined to an armchair upstairs in the family rooms. She knitted and looked occasionally into a Bible which she kept at her side. She was a woman of charm and good spirits and would have made a pleasant hostess, but she was able to come downstairs only once—when her daughter Elizabeth was married in January 1842. Letitia died the following September.

Her daughter-in-law Priscilla Cooper Tyler continued to act as White House hostess, aided by Tyler's three daughters. For social advice they went to Dolley Madison, who knew all the answers. "Should I return calls?" Priscilla asked. "Yes!" said Dolley and that issue was settled.

Tyler was faced with a tougher issue. He discovered that he was not really a Whig at all. He thought the Whigs had given up their old projects—the tariff and a national bank—but they had not. Now he vetoed one Whig measure after another. In protest, his Cabinet resigned, Clay left the Senate, and in January 1843 the House tried to impeach Tyler. They did not succeed, but he was politically lost. During his last years in the White House he did manage to find a second First Lady.

Julia Gardiner Tyler
(1820-1889)

Young Julia Gardiner came to Washington during the winter of 1843. A New Yorker, she had traveled abroad and made a great social splash wherever she went. Her father, a former state senator, took her to the White House to meet President Tyler. She was impressed. So was the President.

Tyler wanted to marry her, but Julia hesitated. The age difference of 30 years seemed a wide gulf.

John Tyler (1790-1862)

In February 1844 Tyler went on a Potomac cruise with a large party of friends and officials, including David Gardiner and his daughters. Their boat was a navy vessel, and several new guns were tested. One of the big guns exploded. Six men were killed, including David Gardiner.

Later, the President visited Julia often, to console her. They were married in New York, in June 1844.

John Quincy Adams told his diary that all of Washington was laughing. If so, Julia did not hear, nor did she pay much attention when her mother wrote to warn her against "display." At receptions in the Blue Room Julia, clad in purple velvet, sat and smiled upon her guests. Standing near her were 12 maids of honor.

Julia adored her husband and her position, and wrote long letters to her mother in praise of both. In March 1845, after eight months of grandeur, she went with Tyler back to his estate in Virginia. There she gave birth to seven children, and took up the cause of the South.

Sarah Childress Polk
(1803-1891)

Sarah Childress was born in Murfreesboro, Tennessee. Her father was a well-to-do merchant. She received a strict religious education at the Salem Female Academy, a Moravian school in North Carolina. Back in Murfreesboro, she met James Knox Polk, a lawyer recently elected to the state legislature. They were married on New Year's Day, 1824.

From the beginning, Sarah kept up a sharp interest in her husband's political life. She helped him write speeches and acted as his secretary. Several years before his marriage Polk had met Andrew Jackson. Sarah liked Jackson—they were "Sally" and "Uncle Andrew" to one another—and Polk himself entered national politics chiefly to help Jackson after the 1824 election. As a member of the House, Polk was one of the Jacksonians who fought against the measures of President Adams. He remained in the House for 14 years, missing only one day of action. He was Speaker from 1835 until 1839.

Then the Polks went back to Tennessee to save the state Democratic party. At Jackson's request Polk ran for governor in 1839. He won the election and again buried himself in work, avoiding parties in fun-loving Nashville. He was not re-elected—1841 was a hard year for Democrats —and he lost again in 1843.

Now and again Polk thought that he might like to be Vice-President. But Andrew Jackson pushed the idea a little further. Jackson felt that Van Buren, the likely Democratic candidate in 1844, was politically foolish to oppose the annexation of Texas. Van Buren feared war with Mexico over Texas, but Jackson was fairly sure that the Democrats would lose votes if their candidate opposed annexation. Westerners and Southerners wanted land, and if Texas was to become a slave state, so much the better.

James Knox Polk (1795-1849)

At the Democratic convention neither Van Buren nor Lewis Cass of Michigan could get enough votes for nomination. Polk's name was suggested, and he was nominated on the ninth ballot. He was thus the first "dark horse" — a relatively unknown candidate whose name is not a household word. When the news got out of Baltimore, people asked one another, "Who is James K. Polk?" With glee, the Whigs took up this phrase as their slogan. Its purpose backfired. The Whig candidate, Henry Clay, lost the election to James K. Polk.

After the election, Tyler's Congress passed resolutions to annex Texas. Tyler signed the bill with a golden pen on March 1, 1845. A few days later, at Polk's inauguration, the golden pen dangled from a chain round the neck of Julia Tyler.

With Julia's last flourish, life at the White House changed. Guided by her religious beliefs, Sarah Polk put an end to dancing, drinking, and card-playing, and she would not see visitors on Sunday. In a deep-toned gown of plum velvet or blue satin, she presided over dinners and receptions with great dignity and a ready wit. People who missed Julia Tyler's waltzes and polkas were usually bored until 80-year-old Dolley Madison arrived, sailing in on the President's arm.

But Polk had little time or taste for parties. He did not mean to run for a second term, and there were certain things he had to get done within four years. Sarah helped him. She was still his secretary, and she read stacks of newspapers and clipped everything that was important.

Congress carried through Polk's plans for an independent treasury and a lower tariff. Polk also wanted the territories of Oregon and California. Oregon he got from the British without a war, California from Mexico after a war. The first shots of the Mexican War were fired on the disputed boundary of the new state of Texas.

In March 1849, a year after the war ended, an exhausted Polk went with Sarah back to Nashville. Three months later he died of cholera. Sarah carefully preserved all of his papers and made their home a shrine to her husband.

Margaret Smith Taylor
(1788-1852)

Margaret Smith was born in Calvert County, Maryland. Her father was a planter and an officer in the army. At his death she went to live with a sister on the Kentucky frontier, where she met a young soldier, Zachary Taylor. A Virginian by birth, Taylor had come to Kentucky at the age of one when his planter father was given a bonus of western land after the Revolutionary War. They settled near Louisville which became the Taylor family home — if only as a burial plot — for Zachary and his wife were on the move soon after their marriage in 1810.

For 30 years Margaret followed him from one frontier post to another, sharing the dangers and hardships of Indian fighting: to Indiana in 1812, to Wisconsin for the Black Hawk War, to Florida to fight the Seminole. In 1840 he was stationed in Louisiana, and they established their first home at Baton Rouge.

By 1845 Taylor was a major general commanding troops in the Army's western division. For a year Taylor and his men hovered near the disputed boundary of Texas and Mexico. In the spring of 1846 President Polk ordered Taylor to march to the Rio Grande, where Mexican troops met him. On land that may have belonged to Mexico or America, American blood was spilled. Polk and Congress declared war. Before the news reached Taylor, he had already won a couple of battles and was ready to move into Mexico.

By the end of 1846 Taylor had taken most of northeastern Mexico. President Polk began to fear that another Whig hero would follow him into office. Accordingly, many of Taylor's best troops were sent to General Winfield Scott who was ordered to invade Mexico City from the coast. On February 22, 1847, near a ranch called Buena Vista, Taylor's 5,000 men were hit by Santa Anna's force of 16,000 to 20,000. Two days later the Mexicans left in mad confusion. Taylor held Buena Vista — and the Whigs had a candidate.

At Philadelphia in 1848 the Whigs were again torn between Webster and Clay. Only a great general could hold the party together long enough to get through an election. Taylor was not very interested in politics and was not eager to be President, but he accepted the nomination. Margaret opposed his nomination and considered the election a deliberate scheme to rob her of a husband.

In November, Democrat Lewis Cass lost votes to the Free-Soil candidate Van Buren, and with the enemy divided, Taylor took the White House. Margaret came up from Baton Rouge and moved into an upstairs bedroom. A semi-invalid, she spent her time knitting. She paid no attention to gossips who claimed she was a backwoodswoman too crude to receive in a public drawing room. At family suppers she came down to eat, and sometimes she appeared at a formal party or reception. But the real task of hostess she gave to her daughter, Betty Taylor Bliss.

Taylor himself, a good-natured host, ambled from guest to guest at summer parties on the White House lawn. His war-horse, Old Whitey, grazed on the lawn and let children pull strands from his tail.

The war that had brought Taylor to the White House also gave his government its biggest problem. The new southwestern territories would have to be slave or free. Congress argued the issue, shouting threats of secession and war. Urged along by Senator Seward of New York,

Betty Taylor Bliss

Zachary Taylor (1784-1850) was called "Old Rough and Ready" by his troops.

Taylor's own political feelings sharpened. He was a Southerner and a slaveowner, but he decided that California should be a free state, and that the idea of secession was nonsense. Others — like Henry Clay — felt that Taylor's bold position risked too much. Clay worked out an elaborate compromise which Taylor might well have vetoed. It never came to that point, for Taylor died of cholera — or a stomach upset — in the summer of 1850. That autumn, under President Fillmore, Congress passed the Compromise of 1850, not as a single bill but in bits and pieces. War was put off for another 10 years.

Margaret Taylor returned to Baton Rouge. When she thought of the White House, all she could remember were the sounds of saws and hammers and funeral music, heard from an upstairs bedroom. She died in 1852 and was buried next to Taylor in the family plot near Louisville.

Abigail Powers Fillmore
(1798-1853)

Abigail Powers was born in Stillwater, New York. Her minister father died when she was young, and at the age of 16 she became a teacher. A few years later, 19-year-old Millard Fillmore came to her classroom. He was a farm boy with a very spotty education. She encouraged

Mary Abigail Fillmore   Milard Fillmore (1800-1874)

him to study. He became a lawyer, settled in East Aurora,
New York, and married Abigail in 1826. Abigail continued
to teach until the birth of their son in 1828.

In 1830 they moved to Buffalo. Fillmore was becoming
active in politics, aided by publisher Thurlow Weed who
was about to form a Whig machine to oppose the Albany
Regency. Weed helped Fillmore enter the state assembly,
and in 1832, the United States House of Representatives.
Fillmore was re-elected, his fortunes rising with the Whig
victory of 1840. In 1848 he was comptroller of New York
when the Whigs placed him on the ticket with Zachary
Taylor.

By midsummer of 1850 Fillmore was President, and
another frail First Lady entered the White House. Abigail
Fillmore's young daughter Mary acted as hostess more
often than her mother. Abigail did make some important

purchases. She ordered a new cook stove, the first to appear in the White House. The cook was confused and angry. Accustomed to a large fireplace, she struggled with the stove for several days, then sent Fillmore to the Patent Office to find out what had gone wrong.

Abigail was dismayed to find no books in the White House. With money from Congress she ordered enough books to start a library. High on her list were the latest novels of Dickens and Thackeray.

Fillmore was a calm, amiable man who wanted to hold together the country, and the Whig party. As Vice-President he had presided over the Senate debate on slavery in the new territories. After Taylor's death, he supported the compromise and enforced its provisions, including a new and stronger Fugitive Slave Law. Northern Whigs were angry about the compromise, and by 1852 they had turned away from Fillmore. At the convention he found himself with Southern support, but that was all. Antislavery Whigs nominated General Winfield Scott, another veteran of the Mexican War. Scott was defeated by Democrat Franklin Pierce, and the Whig party collapsed.

At the inauguration of Pierce, in March 1853, Abigail Fillmore caught a cold from which she did not recover. She died within a month and was buried in Washington. Fillmore returned to Buffalo. He ran again for President in 1856 on the Know-Nothing ticket, and he married again, in 1858.

Jane Appleton Pierce
(1806-1853)

Jane Appleton was born in Hampton, New Hampshire. Her father was president of Bowdoin College. In 1828 she met Franklin Pierce, a young lawyer who was campaigning for Andrew Jackson. Six years later, when they were married, Pierce was a member of the House of Representatives, and in 1836 he was elected to the Senate.

Jane Pierce did not like Washington and she rarely went down to the capital with Pierce. Ill with tuberculosis, she was never more than half-well and found it easier to remain at home in Concord, New Hampshire. She was also very shy, and when two of her sons died as small children, she entered a deep gloom which lasted her lifetime. Many times she begged Pierce to leave the Senate. His work there was not remarkable, and in 1842 he resigned and came back to Concord to practice law.

When the Mexican War broke out in 1846, Pierce hurried to volunteer. He served under Winfield Scott in the invasion of Mexico City, suffered a leg wound, and in

Franklin Pierce (1804-1869)

1848 came back to New Hampshire and the law. By 1852 he was a very important man in the state Democratic party.

At their national convention in Baltimore, the Democrats were split among four possible candidates. On the 35th ballot the name of Pierce was added to the contenders, and he won nomination on the 49th go-around. Another dark horse, he seemed to suit the party's needs in 1852. A New Hampshireman who approved of the Compromise of 1850 could pull votes North and South. Besides, Pierce was thought to be handsome, and people liked his speaking voice. He easily defeated the Whigs' candidate, General Scott — his old commander.

Two months before the inauguration the Pierces' only remaining son, 11-year-old Benjamin, was killed in a train crash. Jane was too ill to come to Washington for the inauguration. When she did make the trip, she brought an aunt to act as hostess, and spent the first two years of Pierce's presidency in an upstairs bedroom. On January

1, 1855, she emerged to attend a White House New Year's party. After that, she often came to state dinners but appeared always to be unhappy.

Under Pierce, the tensions dividing North and South grew sharper, especially after passage of the Kansas-Nebraska Act, which opened up the West to settlers and allowed them to fight out the slavery question among themselves. But Washington society—Northern and Southern—still came together at parties and found other things to talk about. If White House gatherings were dull and melancholy, they could turn elsewhere. The gayest parties were given by Secretary of War Jefferson Davis and his wife.

Pierce was not renominated in 1856. For two years he and Jane traveled abroad, seeking a climate where she might feel well—the useless search of many nineteenth-century tuberculars. On December 2, 1863, Jane Pierce died. Pierce spent his remaining years firing off salvos at President Lincoln, whom he blamed for starting the war. He died in 1869 and was buried next to Jane in Concord.

Harriet Lane, hostess for her uncle James Buchanan, married Henry Elliott Johnston in 1866.

James Buchanan (1791-1868)

Harriet Lane
(1833-1903)

As a young lawyer in Lancaster, Pennsylvania, James Buchanan fell in love with Ann Coleman, daughter of an iron manufacturer. After their engagement, in 1819, they had an argument, and Ann hurried off to the home of a married sister in Philadelphia. She died there, and Buchanan never married. Years later as President he had no First Lady, but he did have a niece.

Harriet Lane was born in Mercersburg, Pennsylvania, in 1833, the daughter of Buchanan's sister Jane. She was a wealthy orphan at the age of nine, and her uncle became her guardian.

Under Harriet Lane the White House again became a fashion center. Above, a reception in the East Room.

When Harriet came to live with him, Buchanan was a United States Senator. He had already served in the House and, as a loyal Jacksonian, had been given a trip to Russia in 1832 to serve as United States minister. In 1844, after 10 years in the Senate, he was spoken of as a favorite son, but he pulled his name out before the convention. President Polk named him Secretary of State. Under

Polk this meant hard work, for Oregon, Texas, and Mexico were Buchanan's problems as much as the President's. After a short rest in Pennsylvania during the Whig years he again tried for the presidency. The winner Pierce appointed him minister to Britain.

Buchanan took Harriet with him. In 1853 she was 20 years old, blonde and blue-eyed. She had gone to the best schools and had known the best people. With her uncle's eye upon the White House, her manners had been perfectly trained. She went through the London social season and met the Queen, who was impressed.

Buchanan was one of few Democrats who had the good fortune to be out of the country during passage of the Kansas-Nebraska Act. One month after he returned from Britain, in the spring of 1856, the Democrats nominated him for President. He was faced by a new antislavery party, the Republicans, who nominated John Frémont, and by Fillmore on the Know-Nothing ticket. The Democrats tried not to talk about slavery. Buchanan won the election though his popular margin was not wide. In 1857 Harriet Lane came with her uncle to the White House and put an an end to years of social gloom.

Harriet threw herself into party-giving with an energy and skill unmatched since the days of Dolley Madison. Flowers from a newly built greenhouse filled the rooms, and new furniture replaced the last of the Monroe pieces. Harriet gave her grandest parties for the Prince of Wales (later Edward VII) when he came to America in 1860. During Edward's visit Buchanan had to sleep in a hallway to make room for the Prince's crowd of traveling companions.

Harriet had a good word for guests from North or South, but by 1860 few people North or South had many good words for Buchanan. At their convention in Charleston, the Northern and Southern Democrats split, and each nominated a candidate. Two more candidates entered the field and in November the Republican, Abraham Lincoln, won the election. Seven Southern states dropped out of the Union, and in Charleston harbor, Major Robert Anderson moved his federal troops from Fort Moultrie to Fort Sumter.

In late February 1861 Buchanan and his niece gave their last reception. General Winfield Scott had already started to move his troops into Washington, to protect the city and the new President.

Mary Todd Lincoln

(1818-1882)

Mary Todd was born in Lexington, Kentucky. Her father was a banker, and Mary was well educated. She was a beautiful young woman with a lively temper. In 1839 she went to Springfield, Illinois, to live with a married sister. In Springfield she met Abraham Lincoln, a lawyer and member of the state legislature. After a stormy romance they were married in 1842, and settled in a boardinghouse in Springfield. A year and a half later, with their small son Robert, they moved into a white frame house with shuttered windows. They were joined by a cow, a servant, and three more sons.

Mary Lincoln was sure that her husband would become President. A Whig, he had campaigned for Harrison in 1840, and national politics began to tempt him. He left the state legislature at the end of his fourth term, in 1842, and tried for the Whig nomination to the House. On his third try, in 1846, he got the nomination. He won the election and went to Washington, where with other Whigs he criticized Polk and the Mexican War. Back in Illinois this view was not popular. Lincoln was sure he could not win a second term, and he did not run for re-election. He campaigned for General Taylor, and came back to Springfield and his law practice.

Mary Lincoln

The Kansas-Nebraska Act of 1854 drew him back into politics. New Western lands were opened to slavery — if the settlers chose it — and all the old attempts to hold the line were destroyed. The sponsor of the Act was Illinois's Democratic Senator, Stephen Douglas. Lincoln spoke against the Act, and in 1856 joined the Republican party and supported Frémont. In 1858 he ran against Douglas for the Senate. Lincoln suggested that they debate, and Douglas picked seven towns where they met before huge crowds during the late summer and early fall of 1858. The election, held in the state legislature (as were all senatorial elections before adoption of the 17th Amendment in 1913) gave the Senate seat to Douglas. Two years later Lincoln faced Douglas again — as well as two Southern candidates — this time for the presidency.

Eleven states had already left the Union when the Lincolns moved into the White House in March 1861. The departing states grabbed as many federal forts as they could. In Charleston, Major Anderson still held Fort Sumter but he needed supplies. Lincoln sent equipment but no additional troops — fair enough, he thought. South Carolina thought not. To that state the shipment was a war-like act, and on April 12, Southern forces opened fire upon Fort Sumter. Four years of war began.

The Republican national convention, Chicago, May 1860. Lincoln was nominated on the third ballot. Other contenders were Senators William Seward of New York and Salmon P. Chase of Ohio.

Mary Lincoln had gained the White House but her stay there was not pleasant. The war would have made party-giving difficult for the most even-tempered, casual hostess. But Mary, whose moods were rarely smooth, took the matter of social leadership seriously. Rivals in the field —like young Kate Chase, daughter of the Secretary of the Treasury—and attacks in the newspapers made the job hard and robbed it of much pleasure. Historians and biographers still argue about Mary Lincoln. Some writers say she was a jealous, nagging wife ready to scream at the slightest push. Others say that Lincoln loved Mary and humored her like a spoiled child.

Two of the Lincoln children came to live in the White House — Willie and Tad. Robert was a student at Harvard during Lincoln's first term, and Edward had died in 1850 at the age of four. In February 1862, 11-year-old Willie died of typhoid fever. Mary was overcome with grief. She went to bed and did not get up for the funeral or to look in on Tad, who was also sick. For months she refused to be cheered. The morning reception on New Year's Day, 1863, brought her before a crowd again. At noon that day Lincoln went upstairs with members of his Cabinet, and signed the Emancipation Proclamation.

The newspapers decided that Mary's long mourning was the work of a show-off. Throughout the war, the press hit Mary on two fronts: for spending great sums of money on furniture and clothing, and for harboring Southern sympathies. To the latter accusation was added a rumor: with so many relatives in the Confederate army, she must be a spy. These charges were quite false, but like the attack upon her spending (which was probably true) they did not improve Mary's mood or temper.

Moods were not always black, however. General Tom Thumb and his bride, both dwarfs, honeymooned in Washington and were given a White House reception. Lincoln and Mary greeted the little people in the East Room, while Robert, home from school, refused to come downstairs. He was not amused.

In March 1864, another general came to the White House. Ulysses S. Grant had won battles in the Mississippi Valley while Eastern generals faltered. Lincoln made him a lieutenant general, and soon after, commander in chief of Union armies.

On April 9, 1865, one month after Lincoln's second inauguration, Grant took Lee's sword in surrender at Appomattox Court House in Virginia. Lincoln had looked ahead to peace in his inaugural address. The North must be ready to treat the South "with malice toward none" and "charity for all." A few days after the surrender, Lincoln asked the Grants to come along to Ford's Theatre to see a new comedy. The Grants had other plans.

Laughing and clapping, the crowd in the theatre did not hear the pistol shot, but they did hear Mary's screams. The gunman, actor John Wilkes Booth, leaped to the stage, ran downstairs, and escaped on a waiting horse. Lincoln was carried to a house across the street, where he died early the next morning.

Abraham Lincoln (1809-1865) with his family:
(left to right) Mary, Willie, Robert, and Tad.

Mary Lincoln went to bed again. She did not come down to the East Room for the funeral, and she did not travel west to Illinois on the funeral train.

Her last years were difficult. Creditors appeared on every side to collect money for gowns and gloves she had never worn. In 1871 Tad died of typhoid fever, at 18. Four years later Robert took her to a sanitarium, where she remained for a year. She was released in 1876 and went abroad to live. In 1880 she came back to Springfield. She lived there with her sister until her death in 1882 at the age of 64.

The Pull Ahead Books

AMERICA'S FIRST LADIES
   1789 to 1865

AMERICA'S FIRST LADIES
   1865 to Present Day

FAMOUS SPIES

SINGERS OF THE BLUES

WESTERN LAWMEN

WESTERN OUTLAWS

PRESIDENTIAL LOSERS

PIRATES AND BUCCANEERS

FAMOUS CRIMEFIGHTERS

We specialize in publishing quality books for
young people. For a complete list please write

LERNER PUBLICATIONS COMPANY

241 First Avenue North, Minneapolis, Minnesota 55401